Kate Noakes lives and writes between Paris and London. Her blog (boomslangpoetry.blogspot.com) is archived by the National Library of Wales and she was elected to the Welsh Academy in 2011. This is her fifth poetry collection.

Previously published books:
Ocean to Interior, Mighty Erudite, 2007
The Wall Menders, Two Rivers Press, 2009
Cape Town, Eyewear Publishing, 2012
I-spy and shanty, corrupt press, 2014

Tattoo on Crow Street

Kate Noakes

Parthian, Cardigan SA43 1ED
www.parthianbooks.com
© Kate Noakes 2015
Edited by Alan Kellermann
ISBN 978-1-910409-99-2
Cover design by www.theundercard.co.uk
Typeset by Elaine Sharples
Printed and bound by Dinefwr Press, Llandybie, Wales
Published with the financial support of the Welsh Books Council.
British Library Cataloguing in Publication Data
A cataloguing record for this book is available from the British Library.

'Tattoos are like drawings, but done by people who can't find any paper.'

A.F. Harrold.

This book is for everyone who ever wanted a tattoo, but is too afraid of needles, and everyone who's already got one or two or three...

Acknowledgements

The poems in this book are mostly about tattoos, their wearers, their stories. Some of the poems travel a long way from the original source. I hope the generous people, friends and random strangers on public transport, in shops and on the streets of Paris, London, Reading and elsewhere, who spared the time to talk to me and bare their skin, are pleased with the results.

I am especially grateful to Jo Bell, Dareka Daremo and James Thompson for long discussions on tattoo whys and wherefores, but who, despite their best encouragements, have failed to get me inked.

Earlier versions of some of these poems have appeared in *Domestic Cherry* ('It comes over me like tropic birds'; 'The Hairdresser'), *Envoi* ('Depali and Raj, Bradford'; 'This old world sting'; 'Now I carry her safe in my arms'; 'Hare dance'; 'Ta Moko'; 'The unmarked girl'), *Ink, Sweat + Tears* ('Exuberance and a girl named Kimberley'), *Magma* ('Circus ladies of a certain age'; 'Some of what she told me'; 'All things weird and wonderful'), *Paris Lit Up Magazine* ('Peacocks Emphysemicly'; 'Dragon and cherry blossom'), *Poetry Ireland Review* ('Tessellation'), *Poetry Wales* ('The Tickle'), *Prole* ('Superman and Lego, fighting'; 'The Copts'), *The Bastille* ('Stella'; 'Indelible'), *Tears in the Fence* ('Jackdaw'), *The Snare's Nest* ('Street Prince'; 'Milk'), and *Upstairs at Duroc* ('Quincunx'). Tattoo in Winter appeared online on the 2012 Poetry Advent Calendar. I thank their editors here.

Contents

How to read a tattoo

I Love song

Tessellation	3
The trellis	4
A cure for the shop assistant	5
Galaxy for an Essex boy	6
The unmarked girl	7
Becoming carrion	8
Crow	9
Jay	10
Going to see the choughs at Aberdaron	11
First bird	12
Depali & Raj, Bradford	13
The lament of the sailor's wife	15
Like a troglodyte spider	16
The Dance Macabre	17
Marie's tattoo	18
All things weird and wonderful	19
Now I carry her safe in my arms	20
Eighteen	21
The posters	22
Dragon and cherry blossom	23
Kitsune	24
Hare dance	25

II Revolution

Superman and Lego, fighting	29
The hairdresser	30
Lucky Jim Rich, the most tattooed man in the world	31

There's no hiding this from your Mum	32
Cicadas	33
Root and branch	35
Iceman, the oldest tattoo	36
Haptics	37
Les mots	38
The tagger's prayer	39
Jackdaw	40
Magpie	41
Street prince	42
This poem wants to be	43
Diary	44
Does your tattoo speak German?	45
The last marked Bedouin	46
Vera for short	47
Murderous crow	48
A Shunning	49
Crow outside the Bastille	50
Being honest with myself	51
The Copts	52
Courage	53
Decalogue	54
Fuck	55
Ta Moko	56
A good enough reason	57
Scimitar	58
There were days when you plotted my body –	59
Katrina and the lily	60
This old world sting	61
Peacocks emphysemicly	62
As annuraaq	63

III What the girls say

Tattoo in winter 67

The snake goddess 68

Stella 69

Exuberance and a girl called Kimberley 70

Indelible 71

Island bohemian 72

Some of what she told me 73

Circus ladies of a certain age 74

Journeymen 75

Quincunx 76

Ex 77

Pig 78

The woman who chose her own name 79

A fish without wheels 80

I should be a wiser fish 81

The Tickle 82

History threatens me with repetition 83

Because of impatience 84

Never settle 85

Taking up archery 86

Milk 87

It comes over me like tropic birds 88

Res ipsa loquitor 89

The tattoo of lost property 90

Pandora 91

End Notes 92

How to read a tattoo

You can't. Ask.
It will speak.

Don't start with assumptions of class
moments of madness, mis-spent youth
consumption of booze, abuse.

What you can't guess is intent
but if you're ready to listen
the tattoo keeper will always be
a surprise.

I
Love song

Tessellation

The best in a while was half-hidden
under the right t-shirt sleeve
of a jazz fan in the Kloof Street Spar.

He was buying a sandwich lunch
crisps, a can of fizzy drink.
I questioned his blank jigsaw

just one tile missing.
His girlfriend, cradling
a two litre carton of juice

supplied the answer, the last piece
inked on her left arm in the place
that when, side by side, they fitted.

I wondered if they'd do something greater
more razzle-dazzle, with those outlines, and later
thought of all his blue girlfriends

in bars, gyms and offices across the city
looking for brave new men with wit
enough to start their puzzles.

The trellis

for Jo

As if to prove that life is complicated
you and I a series of negotiations, boxes

checks and balances, I've drilled a cross-hatch
of grey trellis-work into my shoulder blade.

It's rampant with roses and morning glory
is splashed with ruby blood to make true our story.

A cure for the shop assistant

It was hard, the hardest thing on earth
the hardest thing she'd ever done
admit the man she loved would never
give her a diamond, hopeless, her one-sided love.

It came to her straight and clear, a way to facet
her body with the next level of love.
She drew a brilliant gem as large and one-sided
as hope, found a sympathetic man to cut it in her
in diamond blue, the colour of the hardest thing.

It glints in a birds' nest of musical notes
the hardest thing in the centre of her neck
says more than any one-sided words
she might form for love. At night her heart
her hope, glows where it leapt in her diamond throat.

Galaxy for an Essex boy

Soft. Ink falls. Pre-dawn rain
multiplies gold boy's tattoos in the dark.
They start moving, grow even bolder
mermaids swim lengths, hybrid-roses briar
angels swoop over, clouds tower across
sky's expanse, italics of love and hate
prayer and such deep, deep longing flutter
like plane-trailed "will you marry me" banners.
It's becoming weird, a tapping sound
almost out of hand: one night he falls asleep
with his wife's Hindi name still mis-spelled
next day half the American flag
stripes his arm, the starry half, of course.

The unmarked girl

I am skin-flayed, raw
muscles marbled
with just enough fat to be interesting

meat and sinews fresh-cleaved
from my bones. Which is to say
I am carpaccio

and what I need from you
is mustard, a little mixing
a gentle molding

can you spare me a saffron yolk
to make us melt in the mouth
and worth the eating?

Becoming carrion

Sister crows, too late
I hear death
rattling your throats
and I'm too small
to stop the slaughter.

I can only mourn you
turning my head
from your fence-nailed, splayed bodies
and ripped feathers
autumning the dust.

Ghost crows, you darken
my sight. Your eyes
dulled beads of coal
obsidian, jet, black as
the starless bush night

your beaks gape
for the red wind to sing
its dirges. Sister ghosts
leave the nests to me.
I'm grown enough.

Crow

Crow's first weeks, cemeteries; black Carrara marble
fitted her mood, anchored her, gave her homeliness.
The graveyard gangs at Pere Lachaise, Montmartre

were welcoming; no-one tried to stone her.
Her bent feather started to heal.
All winter she worked on this re-sheening.

Spring, Crow tired of funeral flowers, chrysanths
tasted green. Time to move on alone.
Scanning north she spotted a new park

imported rocks, cascade, pond, people
newly-leaved planes, limes, shelter
the caws of distant males, young ones.

A boy stretched out on the grass, sleeping.
His black hair the first thing she noticed
when he opened his eyes, black too.

His nose had the same curve as her bill
but he was dressed in black, head to toe.
What struck her was rare, so she paced him

made her softest calls, hoping they didn't sound
metallic, grating in her throat. The boy was interested
she could feel his stare on her back.

This watch-pace-dance went on for days
weeks it seemed. Crow nudged the boy
he didn't move. She nipped gently at his chest.

This tickled; he curled up in a smile
nestling Crow in his arms, held her tightly to him.
She sighed and become a woman once more.

9

Jay

You should count yourself lucky
to find one of my feathers along your way

to stoop and pick its barred-blue
from your hard-oak path

have it air and brighten your day.
But perhaps I'm over-preening –

darting about this small wood –
blue-on-blue like Puck – yet know

there are many more to be plucked
if you can just summon up the courage.

Going to see the choughs at Aberdaron

Say it in a nonchalant way as if to the pub
or to read *Libération* in a cafe.

Come along the sand cariad, past the tombs
of the chattering dead and their daily news.

Meet me by the cliffs where my brothers dance in
their red stockings and stab loose slabs of soil for worms.

I'm patient in scarlet boots, waiting. Here I am
new black coat, lips fresh with coral.

First bird

I want you to feel my raw bird energy
the stretch of flesh and sinew.

I'm not a splayed wing, wrenched and bloodied
by the roadside, knuckle-cracked and splintered.

I am real bird. Whole and hungry. Raven.

See how I ravage the land, petrify wood, acres of
first-growth turned stone in the ash of my firebrand.

Watch me laugh for the thrill of it
as my feathers singe and blacken in the smoke.

Here's my best trick: hiding fire in rock, when
you strike two pebbles there's always a spark.

You know this. It's true every time anger
or desire rises in your chest.

That's me love, full and famished. Raven.

Depali & Raj, Bradford

Aunties fuss the way only aunties can fuss, over snacks and tea, making an art of distracting me from a day of sitting.

Surrendering my body is to be a street-sculpture, sprayed silver head to toe: holding, holding, holding the pose. My hands and feet are patterned at the same time; the henna is thick paste applied fine-fine. Syringes kiss, sometimes catch, my skin. It smells of mud like river-bank on washdays, aunties say. It makes them happy.

Paisley is made of peacocks' eyes; their shimmering tail feathers. Dad bought me a feather fan in Bombay when I was five. How many eggs can a peacock lay?

The henna women break to stretch their backs, take just a little something and another cup of spiced cha. Cardamom and cinnamon fill the front room.

I kept the fan in my dressing table for its saffron and street-spice. The cat found it though, ripped it feather by feather into a dust of gold-green and indigo.

Henna is intricate as writing, dots and flowers, black, the same for your hair. It dries fast, has to flake on its own – no rubbing or you'll spoil, bad-bad luck for you, say my sage aunties.

Raj is here in a white turban, smiling. He looks good out of his collar and tie. Tradition suits him. Yes.

Music now and aunties are dancing in kitchen and hall, practising handclaps and ullalahs – Bhangra, Bhangra, Bhangra – makes my head ache.

Dusk, and popadoms are being puffed on the gas. Pots of rogan josh and dahl are warming. Rice won't be long. As sodium lights the net curtains, an aunty declares I am no longer queen. Quick-quick, you are done.

The lament of the sailor's wife

In the Carrib an Aran sweater
is too heavy for a tale of home
so let the blood-drip dagger
hearts, chained anchors
your mother's love, my name
bring you to me again.

Your skin speaks from the Locker
as wool and needle identity
the heavy ring in your ear
is golden passage north to me.

Like a troglodyte spider

I'm not fond of this cave
its cold, its dark, its flowstones
yet I try to make it my home
as I know with time you will crack

the way plate-glass can shatter
into cobwebs spun by my sisters
each weaving their traces
madly trying for a mate

and which with one well-timed
kick will break in spite of safety
and steel and I know
I will not have to try too hard.

The Dance Macabre

The body sings, releases, flows
when it comes to it, this is how to let me go

find a good floor, a versatile band
and hold one another hand over hand

dance me gigs and reels
tap out the night with toes of steel

strip a willow and think of me
my pillowed head spinning free.

Marie's tattoo

New Year's Eve, the cusp of the year
I remember the line running up
the soft side of your arm
a war-time stocking
a gift too silky for your legs.

All things weird and wonderful

In the shade and fade of light, mad-beard man
bums beer and cigarettes with such charm
booze-breaths his rage and wild songs at the sky
us watchers and several passers-by

collides with cat-box girl who porters
a macaw, her gold and turquoise star
clay-licking the bars, and all is quite well
with the Chinaman pushing up the hill

stretching horned toes and Mandarin beard
into a tall tale of the city, heard
by a woman who poses sleeved in frills
the Thursday night Venus of Belleville

sipping her pastis *Aux Folies* alone
save pirates, parrots, skulls and crossed bones.

Now I carry her safe in my arms

for James

Our slender swallow-mother
needed to be alone, fled

                        returned though
rebuilt our nest with earth, her body poured
into the home till winter broke it back to ground.

That was mystery to her who knew only sun
the warmth of summer rain

                        but time, again –
she busied with mud and spit – spent hours
beating out her heart, filled our gold mouths

not one of us hungry in all those years.

Eighteen

Last night I was my grandmother Lil again
scared of Mamgu and her locking me
in the back-kitchen pantry.

My news could not be stored behind rows
of Kilner jars, or dripped into basins of beef fat
not tied up with Johnny Onion strings
or left on marble in the meat safe to rot.

It was not exactly news, or if it was
it was old news, but that's little comfort
against sickness, my waist thickening.

Lil's heart in my throat, my cheeks burn
a ball of cells curls around itself.
My mother is stirring and me with her.

The posters

of the disappeared are ranged
along the security fence
the missing children smile, frown, fade.

Take one at random. Susan
our daughter, who didn't come home
from Glastonbury in 1993.

If you know a woman with a thatch
of dark hair and sparkling eyes
call us, we miss her.

Susan, if you're reading this
we love you. Let us know.
Mum and Dad. xx

A number, a distinguishing mark
on her right ankle
a half-moon and star tattoo.

Dragon and cherry blossom

Pink snow she called it, arms up to catch the petals
falling in our kitchen. My grandmother, a girl in Kyoto.

It was something to hold on to in the broiling hut
when glare and desert dust almost killed her.

The front-yard prunus was turning leaf
the day she returned to Vernal Heights.

She wept as it flowered that first free spring.
And picnicked with my mother in the drifts

munching red bean sweets and loquats
oblivious to passers-by, their silent neighbours.

Blossom could wipe away the past she hoped.
So I chose it for the dragon to scale through

on its way to my chest. She never liked my sleeve
didn't want a gangster grandson

sucked teeth every time I wore a T-shirt, but
couldn't argue with the force of the cherry tree.

Kitsune

for Dareka

Sing me the fox, kitsune
how her power extends down your arms
but don't fear me. Don't be alarmed

I'm not that woman
though you met me alone in the murk
I won't wake you with my winter bark.

I'll be fox in the way
you might sometimes see my tail
hidden, curled around a pearl

only you will be able to tell
if it can burst with flame
and purple smoke, the haze in which I came.

Hare dance

I've seen a dozen hares waltz
on the crooked back of hills
green down to a scudding sea
tango between jewelled gorse
and rocks scoured, pale with lichen.

Our hares are moon-mad quick-steppers
smoothing the fields with wet feet
never northern hares braving
all the snows of all the years
millennia of solos.

I am blind to them, spotted
in their winter coats, cautious
over the crusted land, tapping
for frozen grass and cloud-berries.

In the low rays at afternoon's end
they dance brighter than ice, white
silver, a play of sun on melt-water
as it hurries to the Arctic foam.

II
Revolution

Superman and Lego, fighting

A stranger will start taking off her clothes
to tell you of the lotus flower in the wheel
of life that's stopped spinning
between her shoulder blades; or the koi
treading water on her slim hip
or the band logo on the inside of her wrist
that lead to learning guitar and a year
gigging across America; and that she's glad
she didn't go for the man-faced fish
with hairy balls prominent under its tail
from the book of if-you're-mad enough-
I'll-do-it-for-free; or the two for one offer
on something like Superman and Lego, fighting.

The hairdresser

Behind her ear a scorpion
holds its ground, firm on her neck
ready to impale any hand
that crawls up her back
tail poised, poison tipped
it drips acid into her veins.

Her hoops and sovereign chain
shine on its black carapace
hard gold for a hard girl.
I'm not fooled by a ring
spelling Mum, but I am wrong –

Scorpio's her birth sign
not invitation to a stabbing
makes her loyal, always right
devoted, quick-tongued.
She says she's mellowed
but I'm cautious around her
the scissors near my eyes.

Lucky Jim Rich, the most tattooed man in the world

Look, and tell me if it's true: your skin's so thick
with blue, bruises do not show on you?

There's no hiding this from your Mum

for Zombie Boy

Make up might work for a while
I think you've proved that
but let's be honest, you're not
a shy, retiring chap.

You're not into butterfly –
catch, more death's head moths
blow-fly worms, cock-roaches
insects you can't shake off.

The Rubicon-crossed Simon once said
when you've gone for the face
no way back from here
alea iacta est

but you're one for the circus
limelight, parlour tricks.
No doubt it felt easy
to go straight for the Styx

yet inflation's a bugger
these hard days you know
Charon charges much, much more
than two gold coins a go.

Cicadas

I put dead words on the paper
like stamps licked by other languages
or insects impaled with surprise
by the impersonal rigour of pins.
A question of words, Jose Saramago
translated by Jason Francis Mc Gimsey.

Language is a cicada, tzitzika, emerging
every few years, morphing till there's no
truth to it anymore, nothing that needs
preserving in alcohol lest it lose its colour.
It's all to be used, abused, every
twitch of its tymbal. I try to let it sing
but these days I'm deaf and
I put dead words on the paper.

They're hard as leafhoppers – thud
thump, they pound my brain
with dog-day meanings, the business
of deciphering, the insistence of metaphors
their lies, their not-so-quiet ironies.
I wish they'd be collected with greater
ease and sit quietly, jar-flies
like stamps licked by dead languages

or, spittlebugs, pulped against
the windshield on the road to Land's End
soft-kill of longed-for journeys;
or the blood-eyed locusts from science
after a weekend power-cut, imagos hollow-dead
on lab floor when we opened the cage.
Make them emerald-winged
or insects impaled with surprise

kept on boards with prominent notation
at least for me to admire the way
they breathe through their shells
their clever construction
and their mysterious flight.
I'm feeble at this task: let them moult
and free themselves when held fast
by the impersonal rigour of pins.

Root and branch

Plant pig
choke fig
rock throttler
strangler vine
vast complex
no ripper this time
no sand maker
or boulder crusher
it winds
and binds
ancient stones
in a twisted line
like the one
wrapping you
finger-tip to hair-line
in thick fibres   fine
grafting anger
to your shoulder
keeping jealousy
green on your arm
rooting contemplation's
violet   blue's calm
Isis' way
to hold you
steady   willing   ready.

Iceman, the oldest tattoo

It's for the old ones to point
and show. Only they know now
how the soot-tapped map of dots
and lines on my legs can heal
sore bones and sicknesses
of lungs, heart, head.

They follow the paths still
have named the spots where
good spirits grow strongest
chest's cave, heart's bower, head's grove.
I don't question these ways. I let them
flow over and around me
and wait for winter's damp
in my hips to make itself at home.

Haptics

Fruit. Any variety will do
a russet, citrus or bramble, make it
magnetic, pricked into your skin
anywhere on your body– you choose.
This is the future.

An odd sensation, a pulse, two
your heart beats on your wrist or shoulder.
You're a dog responding to a call, a text.
No more passwords, forget secrets.
This is future.

You can be read like a bag of supermarket fruit
apples, oranges or blackberries
tracked so simply to your rendez-vous.
Glue on your fingers won't erase this mark.
This is bright future.

It can't be seen, this ferrous tattoo
but will be there, always
twenty-four-seven, three-six-five.
You can't downtime your life.
This is future, bright, bright.

Les mots

The difference between us might
in the end come down to something
as simple as five apples on a plate
the first thing you saw lit up
this morning you wanted to paint

so you brushed rosy skin with oil
slicked green on linen
incised them with your palette knife
glossy, tempting till saliva
pooled in my mouth.

But the difference between us
is not my desire to bite into flesh
or yours to render it, no, it's all
in the words: still life
holds out hope in frozen motion
nature morte sounds deadly final.

The tagger's prayer

Give me the strength
to see the purple side of buildings
the green of the road
orange tree trunks

black lines framing
the edges of everything

toilet seats   foetuses   Mexican wrestlers

and the boldness to sign

my name somewhere
anywhere   here   there
everywhere
for all the world to see.

Jackdaw

I'm the left and right of it
where black and white meet and meld
the proof of complication
ambiguous   a compromise
of this and that that and the other

I shade ruins above tidy town
tussock and castle-tumbled stone
ramparts where worms
have worked   composting the midden

I'm the right and left of it
where white and black meld and meet
complication's proof   a compromise
of that and this   the other and that   ambiguous

At wood's edge I'm bleeding light
first rays and long shadows   the start
of chorus and roost   a folded/unfolded wing
out/back from hunting

I'm where black and white meet
the meld of it   left and right
proof   complication   a this   that
the other ambiguous compromise

By ring roads I'm straggle trees
leaf-sooted by fungus   where gall hides
home of hoardings   sodium glare
drive-by place to anywhere.

Magpie

I'm both at once, two-tone
     and I've never been able to see sorrow

don't miss green's shimmer-defining monochrome.
     What is so very dark about my face?

In unlikely places, glass and concrete canyon
     chiaroscuro lacks subtlety

and I can't do this alone, so I'm Mod
     of the gold wood and I need you, mirror-boy

to fight off others, trinket our twiggy nest –
     bring me silver, bring me joy.

Street prince

Phone box boy sleeps in a glass coffin
knees tucked up round his face
the booth steamed by his warmth.

I don't think of him again till the top
of the metro steps at night.

He greets me from under his hood
with an inky hand shakes
coins in half a Coke bottle, says thanks.

He's not my child, but he needs me today
before he curls up
and waits to be buried in the sky.

This poem wants to be

a tattoo that pulses with the heartbeat
taps its iambs to the body's rhythm
snaps with firing nerves
and sweats a little for its rhymes, similes, long lines.

It wants to have its letters tingle when touched
its sensuous words luxuriate
and burrow beneath dry surface ink into living vellum
to be immortal in un-fadeable layers
of derma and fat, remembered as brilliant
survive centuries, millennia; as if

studiously copied out by scribes
itallicised, incised, rendered in gold leaf
its initial letter enameled into a scene of monks
at prayer, all that cant in the face of christ
his mother, his saints, or fanaticism
all that was once hip in Elvis, Marley, Hendrix.

Diary

Which is the more unclean thing
prawn, lobster, swine? Is this worse?

These are only questions when there is a god.
If god is dead, these six digits

forced on my arm are no offence.
I can't hurt something absent.

Does your tattoo speak German?

Mengele was tricky. I suppose
he never thought he'd need to tell his type
unlikely ever to be in a fight.

You can't approach a silver-haired man
drinking coffee in the square
rip off his shirt sleeve and yank up
his arm to check if it's there.

This hunt needs a coterie of heeled
pencil-skirted, professional girls
in 'best uniform' coats
with flattering-old-Nazi skills.

It's only when naked will we be able
to see if they are A, or O, or B.

The last marked Bedouin

By now she thought wars
would be finished
like the tattoos on her face –
tradition best forgotten.

The gunfire is in the west
over the soft red rocks
and in the sandy north, and east
where map lines chart ownership.

She shakes her head
at the un-tented
squabbling over water and oil
survives selling
trinkets to tourists.

She's got it off pat
a touch of leather hand
on a white woman's arm
a flash of gold teeth
questioning origin
and bidding them welcome.

Vera for short

Your tanned neck
I can see thin-sliced
eaten raw
char-cut-erie
but back to the blood
juggling in that vein
its stickiness sweet
in my throat
me draining you again.
I hear you're taking
daily vitamins fortified with iron.
Keep up your strength, boy
while I size your collar
ready it for my knives.
You can call me Vampira.

You can call me Vampira,
ready my knives
while I size your collar.
Keep up your strength, boy
daily vitamins fortified with iron.
I hear you're taking to
me draining you again.
In my throat
stickiness sweet
juggling in that vein,
but back to the blood
char-cut-erie
eaten raw.
I can see thin sliced
your tanned neck.

Murderous crow

I set aside my pen, choose
a more effective weapon

before me a dagger
weighs well in my hand
larger than you think this carving knife

I plunge it deep between your ribs
till your lungs seal and you choke
on coughed blood, spluttering lights

or perhaps a yard long rapier
is the blade to slash your sides
pin your stomach to the wall till gall flows.

No. I'll take a keen poniard, its sharp stick
in and out
of your gut, me, disappeared.

A Shunning

Crow wanted a quick chat with Gertrude
but she and Alice were not making tea for artists
or painting plates the evening she called.

They were out, probably buying a picture
for the nation, or something generous.
Their house was locked against the dark
her mind before the words form.

She contented herself with leaving a message
a scrap of a thing pushed under the door
in the hope of being forgiven. She hasn't
heard. It's been weeks. Nothing.

She supposes she's only to be tolerated now, or
worse. She's thinking of buying a map of Coventry.

Crow outside the Bastille

You're an iron door slammed tight
against the world of you – the one
I want to explore, for better or worse
carbonised, your prison/ mine
rusting now in places where years
water, air have alchemised
exfoliated you in patches, but
you're firm on your hinges
racked and pinioned, reinforced
resistant to my touch.

It will take all my strength,
both hands against your studded chest
to push you open, even if I had the right key.
I wish you were something less solid
wire mesh perhaps, or if a grill is too much
to ask, can't you drill the odd
port-hole for me to feel through
to connect with your flesh?

I want you breathing under my hand
not cold-steeled, in case, god forbid
someone scratches you; it won't be me
my nails are pared these days.
Here, take this welding torch, cut
a circle, let me in with the light.

Being honest with myself

I want us
bare chest to bare chest
and arm-tight
so I can feel your heart
quicken with the press.
I want us to hold
each other like this
breast to breast
naked and open
our ribs rising
and falling as one.
Our heads tip
our eyes close so
that wordless sigh of knowing
passes between us
this is how it should be

This is how it should be
passing between us
that wordless sigh of knowing.
Our eyes close so
our heads tip
and fall as one
our ribs rising
naked and open
breast to breast
each other like this.
I want us to hold
quicken with the press
so I can feel your heart
and arm-tight
bare chest to bare chest
I want us.

The Copts

Cairo – life on the street
in the closed quarters of the city

you might still be able to see
the woman in the cemetery
burning pyres of dead flowers
and feeding arrow-eyed cats

or the obsessive as she sweeps
and washes her thin section of cobbles
sweeps and washes it every day
sweeps and washes it twice a day

or Sebastian, a penitent man, arm
steadied on a rickety table
in the cream-stone sun
ready for a new design.

A cross comes to life in filigree
iron-work forged from his flesh.
He bears it well, laughs, grins to make light
of what might be a last cigarette.

Courage

I highlight, frame, underline, score in black
with a flourish, and sweep, wide and free
over the contours of major muscles.
Your body flexes, my design rests
integral, but there's more to this sum
of blots, however carefully tapped.

Here, ancient luck banishes evil
with one blink, back four millennia
to the source of this magic
I am the eye of Horus.
My deep incantation will keep you
from Nile flood, the hand-chop of war
the plagues of a hundred vengeful gods.

My promise if I am wrong: to wrap you
in another amulet, cotton-cool arms
and flesh on flesh I'll charm you from the mud
where paper plants and slick lotus thrive.

Decalogue

If you sing a name
sing not the lord's
sing not in vain.

If you want to sing
if you want to sing in Malaysia
take not that name
take not the lord's
take not in vain.

Don't let your skin
show that name
show the lord
show in vain.

Fuck

Ai Wei Wei's suntan

Now this, this is a fake, a fake tattoo.
It will dissolve like gum packet patches
when you forget on Sunday in the bath
will fade like henna when winter is through.

This fake is a fuck, a fuck tattoo
documents a day boiling in the sun
branding snow-skin with a red word, a text
that reads fuck but heard means fake, real/unreal
U/non-U, priceless/worthless, old/new.

This, this is a fuck, a fake/fuck tattoo.
No amount of aloe can soothe or cool
its itch, its burn. Read by all, fuck
fuck, it shouts, it shocks, especially you.

Ta Moko

Have you crushed a caterpillar for its colour
or burned timbers to blacken your face?
Has it been chiseled by albatross bone?

No, for you this is can only ever be
writing on skin, *kirituhi*.
You'll never understand that this curve
means the bend of the river as it cuts
through rocks in the valley of giant ferns
where my grandfather hunted as a boy.

You don't know this dot is the best fishing spot
on the stretch of beach where that same river
meets the sea; this forked stick the forest
where my ancestors searched for carving wood,
took kiwi and kakapo to feather cloaks

or these circles are cooking pots handed
from mother to daughter. This sweep is the lie
of our land, unfenced, owned by no-one
our wild place. You see only fashion
a fake-tribal tap, not our stories
and where we are going, nothing sacred.

You've not journeyed beneath the earth for a wife
brought back the skills of ta moko, you've not
turned your soul inside out for all to see.

A good enough reason

This one, she said, pointing
at the pale pastiche
of a Monarch butterfly
pinned to her groin
was the cheapest they did.

I was broke and so in love
with the girl in the shop,
it was all I could think of
to have her touch me.
It's nasty.

It doesn't go with the tribal
swirls on my calf, which don't
go with the cross-bones, skull
and anchor on my arms, or
the arbour of roses on my back.

I began this to cover my scars, but they're
too deep, too silver-smooth, stretch too far.

Scimitar

A curved white ridge
exactly the top lid of an eye
has winked at me for decades.

I kept its stitch-mark lashes
would toy with those spider threads
when I wanted to remember pain.

More than once I've been tempted
to carve it whole, just a quick
blade-sweep towards my thumb

but as with so many things, I lack
the courage to take a knife.

There were days when you plotted my body –

not one square inch unmapped by your lips
or the stroke of your hands.

You knew every contour of my skin, every
fold and fracture of imperfect me

so you might think delta: Mississippi
Amazon, Yangtzee, and yes

this accretion of white veins is something
about swelling waters, the binding of a flood.

Dry leavings now in a pattern of ripped channels
silver roping my flesh, knotting my belly

the lash of a life that ties me to you.

Katrina and the lily

Stargazers, tigers, turbans, there are lilies
of the wood, of the field and scrub
remembrances of valley, meadow, hill

yet the strongest thrives by the roadside
shines above floodwater and broken levees
ditch-lily, swamp-lily, delta-lily

trumpets a little jazz over the drowned city
shines a ray on a chain-link twisted limb
cries a halleluiah, a returning hymn.

Its deep yellow pollen
on so many shoulders and arms
becomes ink-stain, now, for surviving the storm.

This old world sting

I'm not afraid of flute-song in the city night, waiting for air
too heavy with breath before making itself heard
or coming in low on winter cloud.

I'm not scared of this old-world sting
now I see fly-catchers red-breasting the garden
un-phased by me and my spade
I can barely loose soil before they wake the worms

not now I carry them tight on my shoulder
in a nest-box of skin that makes me their pretty one.
their babe in the wood.

Peacocks emphysemicly

The blue god of a thousand eyes
Krishna in bird form,
can afford a little blindness

one tail feather on the calf
of a young woman. Will it bring her
bad luck when she goes indoors?

No way to prove this anymore
than knowing if the pair grating
in Nehru's rose garden are alive

or if the family in Tamboerskloof
bump-start the day on my old
balcony emphysemicly.

As annuraaq

for Patrick

Let's pretend you're caribou; fur on the inside
a living garment.

No, make it seal, cured, chewed into shape
for a new pair of kamiks, set for my needle
and sinuous thread.

And let's pretend that you trust me.

Drink and I'll busy with your face
quick-stitched whorls from narwhale tusk
traces of the paths bears take into town.

You can unpick this pattern, change it for
fox whiskers or white hare paw, but there'll be
scarring, and I may hurt you more.

III
What the girls say

Tattoo in winter

Ink is frozen under layers of cloth
a painted mummy in the permafrost
of the far Siberian plain

stories suspended till spring
though just once in a while, somewhere
unexpected – a Christmas party, say –

colour leaches into light, blood in snow.
Its wearer becomes shaman.
Give her the stick, let her speak.

The snake goddess

First thing most people notice, except perhaps
legmen or naturalists, not for their shape -
ripe peach, juicy-juicy mango, depending
whether gazed on by old punks or Punjabis -
but because they're bared to the world
uninhibited, are my boobs.

It's only then most people, except legmen
and naturalists, already ahead, notice
the serpents scaling my arms, real snakes
insinuated under my skin and often taken
for lively tattoos of my dominion over nature.
True, if by nature you mean men

not to neglect the ones silvering my hair
like Lamia's or the two wriggling
in my hands, but enough smut.
I've heard eight of the world's most
poisonous snakes live in Australia
and there aren't any legmen there either.

Stella

By day she holds rhythm
under her skin in a tracery of stars
thin like the old crescent moon cut
between forefinger and thumb
by a slipshod bone-setter.

Under ultra-violet in a tented field
a cosmos dances on her arms
those particles of white ink
light-footing space.

Exuberance and a girl called Kimberley

I want to be generous, as my feet
are firmly planted in clay and I'm in danger
of disappearing into a big hole
my house is made of fancy-cut
glass and I can be as rash
and foolish as a girl called Kimberley.

Suppose, impatient for death, I dreamed
of the night sky, saw myself
as the goddess Nut, swallowing
and birthing the sun each day
what if I commissioned blue and gold
for all the world to see.

I'd regret it too, one second
after the fifty-sixth star was done.

Indelible

for a school friend who shall remain nameless

Digging in your arm with a compass, its point
journeys through your flesh, its pencil
plots an arc on your hand, because
double Maths on Wednesdays was boring
feels good, but tracing the furrow
with your blue Parker pen made it indelible.

You chose the right place under your watch
so the crooked cross became invisible
except to the very oldest of your friends
the one or two, you now wish
did not have this knowledge of you.

Island bohemian

for the girl with the Pepsi tattoo

Toe-dipper in black Thames water
I want to be a hammock connoisseur
an oiled-skinned devotee, mixer
of the best cocktails this side of the Equator
a swing-slinger, shell-sorter, kelp-flinger
sand-walker, sea-sounder, light grafter
a sampan, taipan, kaftan
silk-wafter, seed-crafter, bar-singer
sought after, big laugher, late-nighter
casual reader of Kafka, film writer
high-rafter, my daughter, dread-noughter
so-softer, sweet-talker, part-lover
part-joker, toke-smoker, no hoaxer
fastlivin' evergivin', coolfizzin', oh yeah.

Some of what she told me

Outside the supermarket is a good place to wait. Its overhang keeps off the rain.

Before there and the Russians, she preferred the corner by the Dim Sum place. Its owner fed her duck-filled dumplings. She even brought out plum sauce. Sweet. It reminded her of grandmother sitting for hours at a red Formica table, folding and pinching a hundred mouthfuls of joy in the steam.

How in another time she lived in the Palace of Heavenly Delights, wore silks so heavy with gold thread their dragons woke her, rustling scales; how head-rest sleep was hard, keeping the crush from her hair, its sweeps and curls as perfect as un-pressed flowers; how she idled the days practising calligraphy or picking up one grain of rice at a time.

That tonight even thigh-length boots can't keep out the bone-cold, and she no longer needs Madame to turn her chin for the next eager man too lazy to find a proper girlfriend, and who won't trouble himself to say anything kind.

Circus ladies of a certain age

Time came when we were no longer stick-thin
had lost suppleness, our waists thick not slim
had forgotten how to spin by our teeth, swing
the high trapeze, ride bare-back in the ring.

We had to think of something, anything
to keep our souls and the coins coming in.

We eyed-up the stupendous side-show gang
the bearded woman and cigar-shaped man
the freaks of nature like the Siamese twins
the babies in bottles, the pig with wings.

When we found it, the rest was as simple
as running a hem with a fat needle

hours, ours in preparation and design
roses, honeysuckle, sweet columbine
courage needed to lower our neck-lines
lift our fringed skirts and flash our coloured skin.

We teased where patterns ended and began
where ribbons wound anchors, butterflies winged.

Drunk roaring men shouted: show us your tits
we smiled, leaned forward, gave them a bit.

Journeymen

I married a man with a pair of scales
a trough and a whole-ground loaf.
He loved me once, but proved too needy
so I watched him bake in the sun.

I married a man with red-must grapes
stemmed on an old twisted vine.
He loved me once, but soon turned sour
so I stewed him in his own juice.

I married a man with a hammer
and an anvil. He loved me once
but slapped and beat me too too much
so I soaked and left him to cool.

I married a man with an old awl
and a boot. He loved me once
but was fond of right-hard kicking
so I left him stub his toes.

I married a man with carving knives
crossed swords below a bull's head.
He loved me once, but filed my tongue
so I hung him to bleed alone.

Quincunx

Figuring five dots – four corners of a square   between forefinger and thumb

one in the centre, set there   has an innocence to it in one version

prisoner in a cell, the mark of a con

in another, find her, follow her   the uses of a woman

finger her, fuck her, forget her   leaves me numb.

Ex

If a tear drop
is a soul
departed
worn under-eye
not in memoriam
but by a killer
to big-up his face
your cheek
should flow
with blue
so many times
have you
cursed me
cut me
crushed me.
Is that a weir
cascading
beneath your beard?
Perhaps it is.

Pig

Pigment
Pig meant
Pig meant something
Pig meant something else
when he added my name
only to cross it out
two weeks later.

The woman who chose her own name

picked Echo to remind herself of home
where she'd return penniless, tired
of Fish camp and climbing the Sierras
wanting prairie towns, stray dogs on corners

it meant her strong-fist speech, her passion for
shouting at glass and steel in canyoned streets
reflected her need for water, those
crisp mountain lakes she watched herself in

mostly it was for her love of a man
who couldn't see her, only the green-black
Celtic knot he'd made her tie in her back.

A fish without wheels

It must have made me harsh
that jack-hammer shaking my head
enough to uproot my teeth, unlash
my skull-bones, unlock my jaws.

I'm no braver than an island woman
with a sea-blue moustache
the scroll-work on my chin
no easy task
that's the point, the pin-point, pain
bravery, my forever mask.

Bare-faced I'd be a young Ainu
no man, no future, no past
a fish without wheels.

I should be a wiser fish

My sense of smell has been fine
more than fine; I've found my way
to Dyfi's shallow pools each time.

So, how to say: half-way I turned west
and swam through a brackish canal
of dissolved smoke

navigated north alone
jumping boulders
looking for a new river to call home.

I'm not sure of my welcome
the local black-mouths
are as dry as Chinook, the wind

that can shake my gravel redd
lift me by a bear's claw
from the cold stream bed.

The Tickle

Most days you slide from my hands
like a brown trout and splash back
into the city's slip-stream with a sharp
slap of your tail.

I know fish can't turn
their heads, but all the same
I watch till you take the corner.

How would you taste
honey, toasted almonds?
I catch myself and wash away
your promise: the film on my palms.

History threatens me with repetition

Mornings, the streets race with water
sluicing debris; no filth or fester
allowed foothold for long, not even
fake muck when the *quartier* turns film set.

What's this then flapping on a grating?

A flounder, the first chokes of blood
form and clot on its gills, its tail flicks
and silvers. It struggles and flattens.
How its glazing eyes remind me of –

your girlfriend fishing for thoughts worth words.
A fresh surge, and oops! there she goes, free.

Because of impatience

A faded, un-presupposing door in a quiet street, no fancy carvings, no brass fittings, blue, once deepest indigo, the colour of the ocean at the edge of a reef, is what first attracted her to the place, has kept Sybil there till wave-worn. It's one door in thousands locking courtyard gardens and workshops from the street, closing the enquiries of those too casual, too uncommitted to their course.

Crow came, chart in hand, seeking auspices and a vision. Sybil held her hand on the high-backed sofa, gave her tea that tasted tangy with iodine. 'Just a sprinkle of powdered seaweed', she added, 'a reminder this far away, where gulls are inland birds'. Crow sipped and strained it with her teeth, but her mouth was not baleened, so she gulped and tried not to retch. 'Tell me then', Sybil commanded. 'That's your job?' 'Give me something to work with'.

So Crow began the history of loving a pied man. When she fell silent, her eyes downcast, Sybil pierced her with violet eyes, seized her shoulders with her claws and moved closer. She searched beyond Crow's irises, moved in and kissed her. Lip to lip now she tasted of the sea. A slick of thick saline filled her throat. Before she choked, Sybil's tongue eased it away. She felt Crow's whole mouth – roof, teeth, gums, twisted her tongue until there was nothing she did not know, had not felt for herself. She withdrew.

'It's enough. You have remembered how, been generous and all-thinking. Not everything is returned. Calm yourself. You'll find someone worthy, but not here, so far from the sea. Look for a man with salt in his beard and scudding clouds in his eyes. He is for you. Truly.' She clapped her hands, broke whatever spell it was. Crow left exhausted.

Never settle

for Griffin

I

The devil's eyes are on this high-backed seat
my bog oak rest by a sweet coal fire
but black wood is never the place to mend bones
and I am river, and cannot settle.

II

When river is full, it starts spitting its load–
fine sand at first, then larger grains, silt bars and eyots
a settling-out of sorts till next winter's spate
shifts everything downstream.

III

Consider the solution to seaward flow, but remember
my best beloved, back in the never-never, before fire
and the workings of the earth, rock was mud, only settled
under pressure as it didn't know anywhere better.

IV

I don't have the wherewithal to settle this dispute
I cannot refute you. All I know is we two should meet
despite the hurt, and if never, then there's no respite
for either of us on this score, ever.

Taking up archery

I can't be the topless parade woman
proud in Market Street,
showing the rest how it goes, the scars
left by disappeared flesh

                          so I yield
to my weak and feeble body
knit a prosthesis to fill my bra, check
my line in the mirror, wish it there.

Silicon breasts pumped quiver
like jelly-fish, are weighed out
giant lychees at a strange fruit stall.
Revisiting the past is dangerous.

I let it go.

The tattoo woman is my ally
she paints me a perfect nipple, tips
two fingers to tense the string.
I pull back the bow.

Milk

Three bottles of thick milk
on the doorstep, day in, day out
my childhood a race against my sister
and clever blue tits to its creamy
gold top; disappointment
on frozen mornings in lollies of foiled ice.

That was when birds were well-fed
before the unkind woman snatched
thirds of a pint from our recess, before
skinny soya, black tea and forgetting Britishness
before I knew my body could bring it
forth, could gorge and tingle, burst
and overflow for a tiny mouth
to sore my nipples into hard fruit.

It comes over me like tropic birds

in a clear sky sudden-dark with cloud
in drops of fat rain trailed in my up-turned mouth
where I carry sorrow as dots and dashes
blue on my tongue.

Storm turns torrent, pours screw-pines from hill
to surf too quickly to spill their seeds
disappears whole villages in a sweep of water while I watch
as if rain is lava not liquid sunshine.

Stripes pattern my tongue
the youngest child, I have the coldest mouth.
My pain is great for those departed
left me alone, shivering, sick.

Res ipsa loquitor

for Sid and Georgina
after Gertrude Stein

Let it be – The thing speaks for itself – Let it, let it, let it –

Let the thing – Let the thing be – Let the thing be itself – Be

it – Be the thing – Be it for itself – Let it speak – Let it speak

– The thing – Let it speak for itself – The thing let it – The

thing let it be – The thing let it speak, speak, speak – The

thing let it speak for itself – Speak the thing – Speak it –

Speak let it be – Speak it be, it be, it be – Speak it be for

itself – The thing speak – The thing let it speak for itself –

The thing be – The thing for itself – Let it, let it, let it – The

thing let it be for itself – For itself let it – For itself let it be –

The thing, the thing, the thing – For itself the thing speaks –

For itself be – For itself be the thing – For itself speak, speak,

speak – For itself speak it – For itself speak the thing – Itself

let it – Itself let it be – Itself the thing – The thing, the thing,

the thing speaks – Itself speaks – The thing speaks for itself –

Let it be.

The tattoo of lost property

House keys, car keys, small change brass and copper,
the keep-box on Dora's back
                                    safely deposited in layers are
the thing that opens the thing, you know
and the clicker that's slipped down the side
of the sofa with yet another pair of glasses
whose twin is often nowhere to be found
like her handbag, which has a life of its own
and is seldom at the foot of the stairs where
she swears she left it next to the disappeared
dog lead, the cheques that need posting
and the DVDs that never seem to find their way
back to Love Film.
                          At the top are the two bent
playing cards that make up the bridge set
a Monopoly die, Captain Peacock and
Miss Scarlet and the letter K (five points)
a blunt Swiss army knife, her grandmother's
wedding ring and another of those things
you know, that open the thing.
It's how she knows where to find them.

Pandora

If you open this box
the most hideous tattoos will fly
into the heads of artists from here
to the far ends and earth will be littered
with goggle-eyed aliens, hobbits
elves, golems and gremlins
faces made into skulls
grim grim-reapers
dots to join, beer, burgers, pizzas
and when or if you slam down the lid
it'll be too late for regrets
and excuses over drink
though a piercing light might wait
in the corners, a laser to erase all horrors.
That is the only hope.

End Notes

The unmarked girl – in Papua New Guinea an un-tattooed person is called raw, as in uncooked meat.

Eighteen – the word Mamgu is Welsh and is pronounced *Mamgee*, meaning grandmother; here the great-grandmother.

Haptics – Nokia filed a vibrating tattoo patent application in the US in March 2012.

Decalogue – Erykah Badu, Canadian R&B singer, was banned from touring in Malaysia in February 2012 over her 'Allah' tattoo.

Journeymen – In France, even after the abolition of the Guilds in 1791, journeymen sported tattoos to advertise their trades.

PARTHIAN

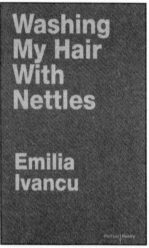

Washing
My Hair
With
Nettles

Emilia
Ivancu

Tattoo
on Crow
Street

Kate
Noakes

Living in the
Delta

new & collected poems

Landeg White

Book of
s o n g s

Norman Schwenk

POETRY